Calamity Jayne

My Hit and Miss Guide to Family Food

Published by Stacey Broadbent

Copyright © 2016 Stacey Broadbent

Licence Notes

This book is licensed for your personal enjoyment only. This book may not be re-sold or given away to other people. If you would like to share this book with another person, please purchase an additional copy for each recipient. If you're reading this book and did not purchase it, or it was not purchased for your use only, then please return to your favourite book retailer and purchase your own copy. Thank you for respecting the hard work of this author.

Photography by Tegan Clark

ISBN: 978-0473429676

About the Author

Hello and welcome to my "Guide to Family Food" I am Calamity Jayne and I'll be your cookery advisor this evening.

For those of you who aren't familiar with my work, I have a blog (www.calamityjaynefoodie.blogspot.co.nz). I have been writing this for the better part of three years now, and thoroughly enjoy sharing my adventures and mishaps in the kitchen.

This all came about as a suggestion from my sister, who had faith in me and my cooking. My very first blog was about the mishaps I had whilst attempting to make her birthday present – let's just say, it did not come out as planned.

Once I had written that and had people comment on it, I was hooked! It is my love of cooking and experimenting that prompted me to write this book for you lovely readers out there, in the hopes that I may inspire someone else to take the journey that is ... food!

I have a deep love not just for food, but for the reaction I get when showing off a new creation. There's nothing quite like the feeling of contentment that comes with making others happy by bringing them something you just whipped up in the kitchen.

I began baking at a young age. Every Sunday my sister and I would help our grandmother bake gingerbread men, cookies and cakes. We would make our own ice cream sundaes, and mix together the cinnamon and sugar for our toast. It was great fun! My grandmother is probably the reason I love cooking so much. She taught me a lot.

Now that I am a mother myself, I love to make cute cupcakes for the kids' parties, and sometimes for no reason at all other than, to bake. I am constantly trying out new recipes and my family get to be the guinea pigs! They love it really!

So I invite you to join me as I show you some of my favourite recipes to share with your family and friends. Simple dishes that will make people go "Wow!"

Stacey

Contents

Baking
Tan Square	11
Rocky Road	13
Chocolate Fudge	15
Truffles	17
Raspberry and Dark Chocolate cupcakes	19
Sugar and Spice Cookies	21
Banana Cake	23
Coffee and Pecan Cake	25

Snacks
Bacon Wrapped Apricots	29
Cheesy Bread Dip	31
Cheese and Pineapple Rolls	33
Vegetable Rolls	35

Dinner
Nachos	39
Fettuccine with Bacon	41
Salmon and Spinach Quiche	43
No Pasta Lasagne	45
Simply Salad- Lettuce Salad	46
Potato Salad	47
Salmon Filo Rolls	49
Couscous Patties with Yoghurt Garlic Dressing	51
Chorizo Risotto	53
Pork Meatballs	55
Spaghetti Bolognese	57
Mini Pizza	59

Desserts
Apricot Pie	63
Pavlova with Chocolate Mousse	65
Homemade Ice Cream	69
Chocolate Cheesecake Pie	71
Ambrosia	73
Semifreddo	75
Rhubarb and Apricot Crumble	77

A few tips before you get started

I always use fan bake when baking so all recipes are made using this unless stated otherwise.

When baking, unless using silicone bakeware, you should always line first to ensure mixtures do not stick and are easily removed.

You should generally have food in the centre of the oven unless stated otherwise.

Teaspoon measurements are 5ml.

Tablespoon measurements are 15ml.

Cup measurements are 250ml.

Baking

Here are some easy to follow recipes to share with family and friends. Keep your cupboards stocked with these goodies and you won't be able to keep the visitors away!

Tan Square

This is the one recipe that I get the most requests for. It is one that was passed down to me from my Mum, and I thank her for that!

If you love a creamy caramel, then this is the slice for you. It honestly beats anything you will buy from a bakery.

Yes. It is that good!

Now in my experience of making this, I have found that the condensed milk you use, makes a huge difference.

Not to the taste, but the texture and overall appearance of the slice itself. The best one to use is Nestle Highlander Condensed Milk, as this is the only one that seems to set. If you don't mind your caramel dribbling down all over your fingers as you try to devour it in a civilised manner, then by all means, try another brand. If you prefer to take your time and enjoy your food, then I suggest you use the tried and true one.

Base
175g Butter
3 C Flour
1/2 C Sugar

Caramel
100g Butter
1 Tin Condensed Milk
2 Tbsp Golden Syrup
1 tsp Vanilla

To make the base, cream butter and sugar. Add flour.
The mixture will be crumbly so don't worry – you're doing it right!
Press ¾ of mix into a greased and lined slice tin. Smooth the top with the back of a spoon.
In a saucepan, combine the caramel ingredients and over a low heat, stir until butter has melted and all is combined. Do not let it boil.
Pour caramel over base, spread it to cover completely. Sprinkle the remaining dough on top – use as much or as little as you like.
Bake at 180°C until golden brown and bubbling around the edges.
(approx. 15-20mins)
Leave to cool in the tin before slicing. Keep in the fridge.

*If you have used one of the brands where it doesn't set, you will need to keep slice in its slice tin and cut as you require it, otherwise, you will end up with shortbread swimming in caramel – not that that's a bad thing!

Rocky Road

There are so many recipes out there for Rocky Road, and I have tried a lot of them! What I have ended up doing is taking bits from them all and making my own combination that works well. The family thinks it's pretty good too!

What is here can be used as a guideline, and you can pick and choose ingredients that you like, and make it your own.

I like to use a combination of different chocolates, but it works just as well with only one variety. The choice is yours.

300g Dark Chocolate
300g Milk Chocolate
2Tbsp Butter
2Tbsp Golden Syrup
2 x Turkish Delight bars
½ C Rice Bubbles
½ C Raisins
½ C Dried Apricots
70g Pecans/Almonds chopped
½ C Mini Marshmallows

Grease a 20cm square tin and line with baking paper – greasing beforehand helps to hold the baking paper in place and stop any bits that may go over the paper from sticking.
Place chocolate, butter and syrup in a bowl and place over saucepan of simmering water – do not let the water touch the bottom of the bowl. Stir until it is melted and smooth.
Chop Turkish Delight, apricots and nuts of your choice. Place in a large bowl with the rice bubbles (or you can use cornflakes), raisins and marshmallows.
Pour the melted chocolate in and stir immediately.
Spoon into your prepared dish and smooth over. You can sprinkle some 100's and 1000's or chocolate hail over top as well if you like.
Place in fridge until firm. Cut into slices.

*This is very sweet so you only need small pieces.

Chocolate Fudge

Who doesn't love a good chocolate fudge??

Now you may have tried to make fudge in the past and ended up with a grainy textured tray of sickly sweet "fudge" but I assure you, this recipe is not in any way like the others.

It is lovely and smooth and there's none of this business of boiling until "soft ball stage".

This is quite simply, a very easy to make, and delicious to eat recipe.

1 Tin Condensed Milk
2 C Dark Chocolate
1 Tbsp Butter
Your choice of orange zest or 1 tsp flavoured essence

I like to use orange zest with this recipe because I think the choc orange flavour is divine. If you prefer you could use peppermint/coffee/raspberry whatever you like.

Melt chocolate in a bowl over saucepan of simmering water.
Warm condensed milk and butter.
Take off the heat and add the melted chocolate and zest/essence.

*If you add zest/essence directly to chocolate, this will start to seize so you will need to work fast and beat the whole mix with a spatula until smooth.
Pour into a lined 20cm square tin and set in fridge.

*I like to put white chocolate buttons on top for decoration, this way you can cut into squares around each button.

Truffles

This is another of those recipes that has so many variations to it. You can add essences for a different flavour, or roll them in chopped nuts for a bit of crunch.

Truffles are super easy to make, and yes you might get a bit messy, but isn't that the fun of baking?

1 C White Chocolate
2 Tbsp Cream
Pinch of Salt

This is so easy! Place all ingredients in a microwave safe bowl and heat for 30 seconds. Remove and stir. Heat again for 20 seconds and keep repeating until you have a smooth consistency. Should only be two or three extra heats.
Cover and place in fridge for at least 3 hours.
Remove from fridge and roll into teaspoon size balls. You can leave them as they are, or roll in chopped nuts, chocolate hail, grated chocolate...

Another option: if you freeze the balls you could then dip them into melted chocolate (perhaps dark choc) to give a chocolate crust.

*These are also great for making hot chocolate with – keep them in the freezer and bring out when needed – add to a mug of milk, heat in microwave for 2 minutes, stir and enjoy!

Raspberry and Dark Chocolate Cupcakes

We grow our own raspberries at home and there are always plenty available to eat. I developed this recipe to use up some of those extra ones.

As you have probably guessed from previous recipes, I have a soft spot for chocolate, in particular, dark chocolate. Berries and chocolate complement each other nicely.

I have used fresh berries, which I think works better, but obviously if they are not in season, you could use frozen ones. Just be prepared for a wetter mix that will need to be eaten sooner.

100g Butter
½ C Caster Sugar
1 tsp Orange Zest
1 tsp Vanilla Paste
1 Egg
1 ½ C Flour
1 tsp Baking Powder
Pinch of Salt
¼ C Milk
1 C Raspberries
½ C Dark Chocolate

Preheat oven to 180^0C
Line cupcake tin with cases.
Cream butter and sugar. Add egg, zest and vanilla, and beat until combined and smooth.
Sift flour, baking powder and salt into a separate bowl.
Add alternately with the milk.
Fold in the raspberries and chocolate – do this gently so as not to crush the berries too much.
Sprinkle a little Demerara Sugar over top to add a bit of crunch.
Bake for 20-25 minutes, until golden around the edges, and centre bounces back when touched.
Leave to cool in tin for a few minutes, before turning onto a wire cooling rack.

Sugar and Spice Cookies

You can't have a cookbook without some form of cookie in it.

There is something about homemade cookies that is just so comforting. Whether you like them dipped in a hot drink of tea or coffee, shared with a friend, or as a quick "on the go" treat as you run out the door, there is a cookie out there for everyone.

These ones are simplistic, with a taste that reminds you of childhood memories – Grandmas kitchen.

75g Butter
1 Egg
½ C White Sugar
½ C Brown Sugar
½ tsp Baking Soda
1 ¼ C Flour

Preheat oven to 180^0C
Cream butter and sugars together. Add egg and beat until well combined.
Fold in flour and baking soda.
Roll into balls about teaspoon size.
In a small bowl combine 2tsp cinnamon with 1Tbsp sugar.
Roll cookie balls in the sugar and spice. Place on baking tray and flatten slightly with a fork.
Leave room as these will spread.
Bake for 10-15 minutes until golden.

You can take them out slightly earlier to get the softer chewier texture, or leave them a little longer so they are crunchier.

Banana Cake

I think everyone needs to have a banana cake recipe on hand. Especially if you have children. If you are anything like me, you will have a constant supply of bananas for quick snacks for the kids. Sometimes they ripen faster than they are eaten and that's when a banana cake is born!

A hint for those of you who always have leftover bananas and maybe don't have the energy to bake, keep those bananas. Pop them in the freezer as they are, then you can defrost them when you feel the need to bake. We don't want anything going to waste!

125g Butter
¼ C Sugar
¼ C Muscavado Sugar
3 Ripe Bananas
1 tsp Vanilla Paste
2 Eggs
75g Ground Almonds
1 ½ C Flour
1 tsp Baking Powder

Preheat oven to 180^0C
Cream butter and sugars together. Add egg and vanilla and beat again until well combined.
Break the banana into chunks and add to the mix, fold in gently.
Sift dry ingredients and fold in.
Pour into cake tin and bake for 45 minutes, until inserted skewer comes out clean.
When cool, sprinkle with a little icing sugar before serving.

Coffee and Pecan Cake

This is one of my favourite recipes to make. You might want to make a double batch because it will go fast! Such a divine taste, and goes great with a hot cup of coffee. I like to use Pecans in this one, but I've also made it with hazelnuts and walnuts.

2 C Self Raising Flour
1 1/4 C Brown Sugar
70g Pecans chopped
1 Tbsp Coffee
1 Tbsp Boiling Water
1 C Milk
2 Eggs
1 tsp Vanilla Extract
150ml Canola Oil

Preheat oven to 180^0C
Sift flour into a large bowl. Add sugar and chopped nuts.
In a jug, mix coffee with boiling water, add milk, eggs, vanilla and oil.
Pour wet ingredients into dry and fold gently.
Pour into a 20cm round cake tin and bake for 45-60mins until the centre bounces back when touched.
Leave in tin for 5 minutes before turning onto a wire rack to cool.
Top with Coffee Buttercream.

Coffee Buttercream

100g Butter softened
1 tsp Vanilla Extract
2 tsp Coffee
1 Tbsp Boiling Water
1 3/4 C Icing Sugar (approx.)
To make butter cream, combine coffee with water.
Beat butter with vanilla and coffee mix until creamy.
Add sugar 2 Tbsp at a time until thick. Increase beater speed and beat until light and fluffy - approx. 3 mins
Spread over cake and top with chocolate hail.

Snacks

This section contains some of my favourite recipes for serving up as side dishes, pot luck platters, and birthday parties, or just for an indulgent snack.

Bacon Wrapped Apricots

The title says it all, doesn't it? Nothing beats the deliciousness of bacon, add to that some plump alcohol (or juice if you prefer) soaked apricots, and you have a winning combination. This is another dish that will really impress people, and requires little effort! I actually serve this alongside our Roast Turkey at Christmas time – the sweetness of the apricot really complements the turkey.

12 Dried Apricots
4 Rashers Streaky Bacon
Schnapps/Orange juice

This is one of those recipes where it's better if you plan ahead. If you know you are going to make them, then allow a few days of soaking. If however you decide to make it on the same day, then even a few hours of soaking is better than nothing.

So basically, put your apricots in a small glass bowl. Pour in schnapps (Sour Apple or Peach are good) to just cover them. If you don't want to use alcohol then orange juice would work just as well. Cover with cling film and leave to soak. I like to give it a stir up each day to make sure that everything is getting a good soaking.

When ready to cook, preheat frying pan to medium heat.
Cut rashers into thirds and wrap each apricot in a portion of bacon, making sure the join is on the wider part of the apricot.

Put in the frying pan, join side down. Pour any leftover alcohol over the top and let them cook for 5 – 10 minutes until starting to crisp up. Turn to the other side and cook for a further 5 - 10 minutes.

It's best to let them rest a little before serving as they are really hot! Being the size that they are, people tend to pop the whole thing in their mouths and a burnt mouth is never a good thing!

Cheesy Bread Dip

Cheesy bread dip always goes down a treat. What's not to love?? A bread case with a hot, gooey, cheesy dip for your crackers or selection of vegetables. Mmmmmmm!

I first tried this about 10 years ago and fell in love with it. I have adapted the recipe several times, depending on what ingredients I have to hand. This is the one I have chosen to share with you.

1 Loaf Unsliced Bread – Vienna is good
250g Cream Cheese
250g Sour Cream
Diced Bacon
1 Orange/Red Capsicum
1 Green/Yellow Capsicum
Garlic Pepper
2 Tbsp Mayonnaise
Spring Onion

*If you want it even cheesier then you can replace sour cream with another tub of cream cheese, or add some extra grated cheese to the mix.

Preheat oven to 150^0C
Carefully slice the top of the Vienna loaf off – don't cut too far down as the loaf is the basket for the dip. Scoop out the inside of the bread – you can keep this for dipping also.
In a bowl, combine the cream cheese and sour cream with the mayonnaise.
Chop the capsicum into small chunks, slice the spring onion, and add these to the cheese mix. Fold in the bacon.
Season with garlic pepper and salt if needed.
Scoop the mix into the prepared bread basket – you want to pack it in with a spoon so that the whole basket is full. Place the bread lid back on.
Wrap in tinfoil and place in oven. Bake for 2 hours.
Remove from oven and tin foil and serve with a platter of crackers and vegetables, and the inner of the bread if you like.
You can always drizzle the bread inner with a little oil and bake before serving.

Cheese and Pineapple Rolls

Oh so gooey and full of creamy goodness!

I love these! What more can I say? Perfect for a plate to take, or an alternative lunch option, or perhaps just a sneaky indulgent snack. Either way, you will not be disappointed.

I use toast bread to make these as it is thicker and can absorb some of the liquid, but if you want to try it with sandwich bread then by all means go for it!

Bread
Onion Soup Mix
Tasty Cheese
Small Tin Crushed Pineapple
1 Tin Reduced Cream

I like to chop off two crusts (opposite sides) on each slice of bread, but you can do it without any crusts if you prefer.
You can also roll it with a rolling pin first, but I don't see any necessity for this.
In a bowl, tip in reduced cream and onion soup mix. Combine with a fork.
Spread a layer on each slice of bread, followed by a small dollop of pineapple (drained) along one edge, and a sprinkle of tasty cheese.
Beginning at end with pineapple, roll up and secure with a toothpick – I find it is easier to push it in on an angle to hold it tightly.
Place on baking tray and brush with a little butter. Continue with every slice.
Bake at 180^0C until golden – about 15 minutes.

*Make sure not to pile too much filling in, it makes it harder to roll and you end up losing a lot of the good stuff. They have plenty of flavour without having to heap it up.

Vegetable Rolls

This is a great thing to make if you have guests who don't eat meat. I think it's always a good idea to have a few vegetarian recipes that work. It's also a great way of getting vegies into your kids without them noticing!

Full of flavour that even the biggest meat-eaters will be hard pressed to find fault with these.

I like to serve them with a bit of Sweet Chilli Sauce on the side.

2 Sheets Puff Pastry
1 Small Potato Peeled
1 Carrot
1 Courgette (I Don't Peel It)
1 Onion, Finely Diced
1 Small Wedge of Pumpkin
1 C Tasty Cheese
2 Tbsp Cream Cheese

Cut your veggies up finely, you could even grate some, but I like the chunks.

Preheat oven to 200^0C
Put the potato and pumpkin in a small saucepan and boil for a few minutes to soften.
Put the carrot, courgette and onion into a frying pan with 1Tbsp butter. Cook for a few minutes until softened and a little colour on them.
Drain potato and pumpkin and add to frying pan for 1 minute.
Transfer to a bowl and season with salt and pepper. Allow it to cool a little. Add cream cheese and tasty cheese and mix to combine. Add more cheese if mix looks a little dry.
Spoon mix onto pastry sheets – spread along one edge leaving plenty of room for rolling. On the opposite edge, brush a little milk. Roll up and press to seal. Repeat with second sheet.
Cut into 1" slices and transfer to baking sheet. Stab with a fork and brush with milk.
Pop in the oven for around 15 minutes or until golden and puffy.

Dinner

THE MAIN MEAL OF THE DAY. IF YOU GET BORED OF HAVING THE SAME OLD MEALS EVERY WEEK THEN THIS IS THE SECTION FOR YOU. THESE ARE SOME OF MY FAMILY'S FAVOURITE MEALS TO ENJOY. A LITTLE TWIST ON TRADITIONAL "FAMILY FOOD".

Nachos

This is my son's absolute favourite meal! I have tried several different varieties, but this seems to be the best one. It's a little more expensive to make, but well worth it. It's a "must have" for all those meat-eaters out there.

If nacho chips aren't your thing, then crisp up some tortillas and cut into wedges, or just serve it up on toast.

Delish!

Nacho Chips
Grated Cheese
5 Rashers of Streaky Bacon
400g Mince
Tin of Chilli Beans
Tin of Tomatoes
½ Onion, Diced
Salt and Pepper

Heat a pan with a drizzle of oil in it. Add bacon and onion and fry until onion has softened and bacon is starting to crisp.
Add mince and brown.
Season with salt and pepper, then add in the chilli beans and tomatoes. Simmer until well combined and juice has reduced slightly.

Arrange nacho chips around plate and spoon meat mix into centre.
Top with grated cheese and pop under the grill for a few minutes – until cheese has melted.
Serve with a generous dollop of sour cream and avocado mashed with a little lemon juice

Fettuccine with Bacon

This can be made with both fresh and bought pasta. If you are lucky enough to have a pasta machine, then I recommend making it fresh. I use two eggs and 1 Cup of flour per person. Do it straight on your bench – pour flour down first and make a well in centre, add eggs to the well. Using a fork, whisk, slowly incorporating the flour as you go. When the "bowl" is almost to breaking point, use floured hands to combine and knead. Wrap in cling film and leave for 30mins before putting through machine and making your fettucine.

I prefer the taste and texture of fresh pasta, and find it more filling than the packaged stuff. But if making it isn't your "thing" then totally go with the bought stuff. Just know that you are missing out!

Fettuccine
5 Rashers Streaky Bacon
1 Onion diced
1 C Peas (frozen is fine)
Knob of Butter
Good White Wine
Parmesan Cheese

Heat pan with a little knob of butter. Add onion and bacon and fry for around 5 minutes. You want the onions to be soft and the bacon to be coloured, not necessarily crisp.
While this is happening you need to boil a large pot of water. Once boiling, add a good pinch of salt (don't be stingy here). Add pasta – if fresh it will only take a few minutes and will rise to the top when ready.
Add peas to the bacon pan and cook for 1 minute.
Add a good splash of white wine and allow to reduce down – only a few minutes.
Drain pasta – reserving some water in case pasta gets claggy.
Add to the bacon pan and toss well. Add another dollop of butter and a good sprinkle of parmesan.
Toss again. If it looks to be too sticky, then add a little of the cooking water and toss again.

Serve up with an extra sprinkle of grated parmesan over top. Drizzle a little olive oil over and enjoy!

*If parmesan scares you a bit, then try adding just a small amount at first – I always had a problem with parmesan until I tried it in my pasta and now I don't make pasta without it. It adds so much flavour and you only need a little amount. Don't be scared!

Salmon and Spinach Quiche

I like to use couscous as my base for this recipe. It only takes a few tablespoons to soak up the liquid and form a suitable base. And it's not as fatty as pastry. Bonus!

I also recommend using the salmon slices rather than the tinned stuff. It will still work with it, but the taste is so much better, and the colour more vibrant. One pack of 100g Salmon slices will normally do us for two quiches so it goes quite far, making it quite a cheap meal to make.

2 Tbsp Couscous (per quiche)
100g Salmon Slices
Spinach (fresh baby, or frozen is fine)
Approx. 10 large eggs
1/2C Cream Cheese
1/4C Cream
3/4 C Grated Cheese

Sprinkle your quiche tins with the couscous – it doesn't need to cover it, as it will expand once all the liquid is in with it.
Arrange salmon around the dish. You can leave it as big chunks or break it up smaller.
If using frozen spinach – it will need to be defrosted first, then give it a gentle squeeze to release all the extra water. Separate and spread around the dish.
I like to add blobs of cream cheese around the salmon pieces.
In a jug, put about ¼ C cream cheese – room temperature, add eggs and cream and beat. Season.
Pour into your dish. It needs to just cover the other ingredients to work best.
Sprinkle with grated cheese and pop in the oven at 180^0C until golden and set in the centre. About 20-30 minutes.

*Optional Extras - Add grated carrot or courgette to the egg mix before pouring into the dish.

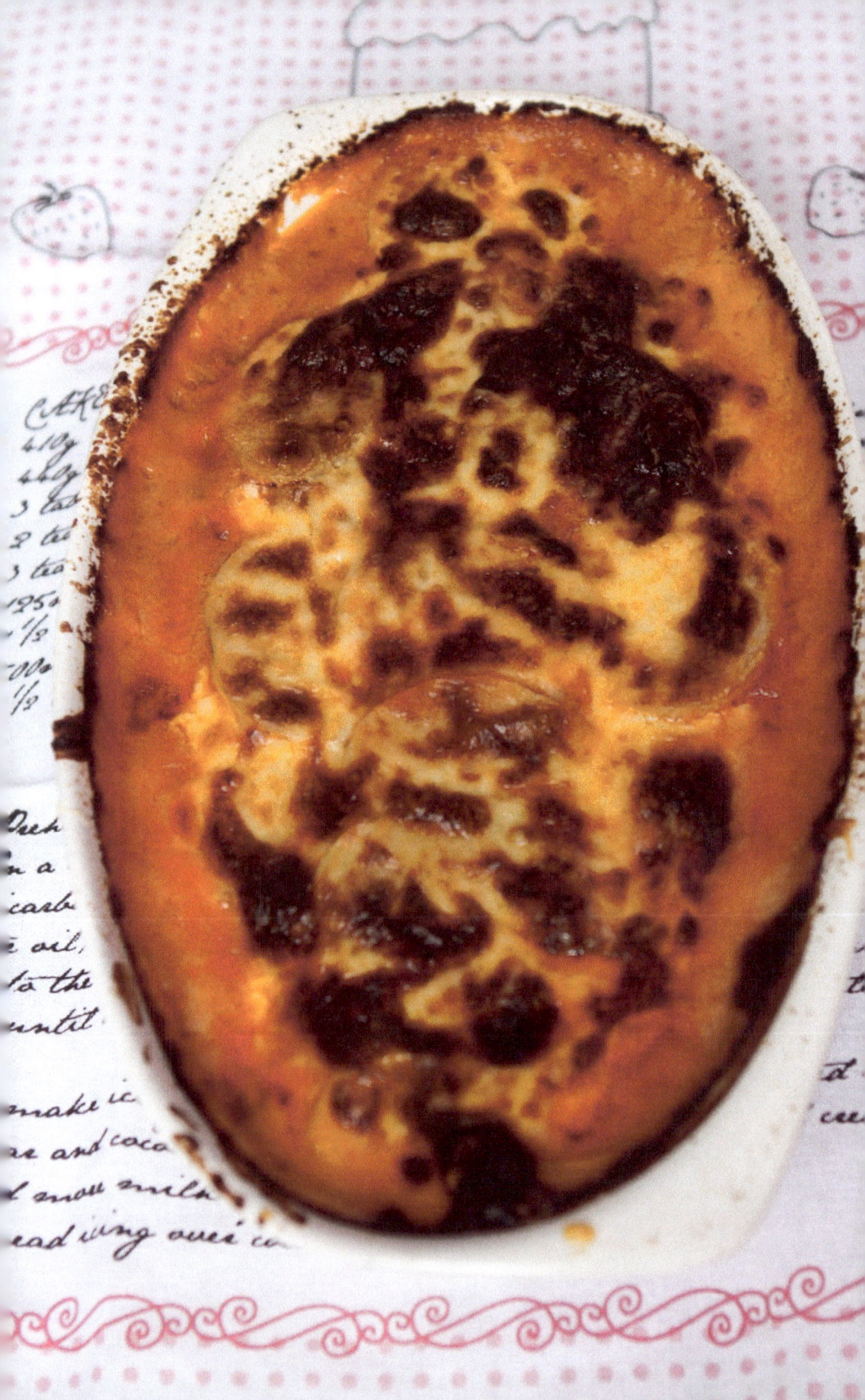

No Pasta Lasagne

Now, I am a big fan of pasta as you well know, but sometimes you just want something different. You may have some spuds in the cupboard that have seen better days, and need to be eaten. This is a great way to use up those leftover odds and sods you have lying around.

2 Large Potatoes, Washed
500g Mince
1 Large Carrot
1-2 Courgettes
Tin Tomato Puree
1 Onion Sliced
1 C Milk
1 Tbsp Butter
1 Tbsp Flour
2 C Cheese
3 Tbsp Parmesan
1x Onion Soup Mix

Wash and slice potatoes into 5mm slices.
Heat oil in a pan, add sliced onions. Cook until softened then add the mince. Break it up and brown it all over. Season with salt and pepper.
Grate carrot and courgette and add to the pan with tomato puree and soup mix. Simmer for 10 minutes.
In a small saucepan, heat the butter, once melted, add flour and stir. This will be thick. Keep stirring as you slowly add the milk.
If lumps form then whisk it until smooth.
Continue stirring until it begins to thicken – remove from heat and add 3/4 C cheese.
In a large greased dish assemble the lasagne – 1/3 mince mix, layer of potatoes, season with salt and pepper, 1/3 C cheese, repeat layers. On the last layer, pour cheese sauce over the potatoes before sprinkling with the last bit of cheese and grated parmesan.
Bake in oven at 200^0C for 45 minutes. Cheese should be bubbling and golden.
Allow to rest for 5 minutes before slicing and serving.

Simply Salad

Once the summer sun starts warming us and the barbeques are wiped down in preparation for the "outdoor dinners", you need to have a couple of yummy salad recipes to bring out. It can get boring having the same old salad day in, day out, so I thought "Why not include some twists to brighten up the humble salad?"

Lettuce Salad

Lettuce of choice, I like to use the frilly "fancy" lettuce
1 Apple
Four slices of cheese cut into chunks
8 Cherry Tomatoes cut in half or 2 tomatoes cut into cubes
½ Capsicum, Chopped

Rinse lettuce and put through a salad spinner if you have one (really does make a difference to your salad). Break into smaller pieces and add to your bowl.
Slice apple into fat matchsticks, add to bowl with other ingredients.
You can use grated cheese if you prefer, but I quite like the chunks.
Season with salt and pepper. Drizzle 1 ½ Tbsp Olive Oil and 2tsp Balsamic Vinegar over and toss to combine.

Potato Salad

3 Large Potatoes or a dozen new potatoes chopped into bite-size chunks
2 Eggs
½ Capsicum Chopped
8 Cherry Tomatoes cut in half or 2 tomatoes sliced and cubed
Spring Onion
½ C Corn Kernels
2 Tbsp Mayonnaise
Salt and Pepper

Boil potatoes with the eggs until potatoes are cooked but still firm. Drain. Run under cold water to remove any starchiness.
Slice eggs into chunks.
Combine all ingredients in a bowl. Stir through the mayonnaise and season with salt and pepper. If you have garlic pepper, then this makes a delicious aioli type flavour.

Salmon Filo Rolls

Growing up, I was never a fan of salmon. I actually didn't take a liking to it until my wedding day! My husband is a seafood lover so I made sure there was some present for our meal. The chef we had was amazing and he converted me! I now love a good bit of salmon. Our kids do too which is great. This is probably my favourite recipe to make with it. It can be a bit fiddly, but once you get into a rhythm, it doesn't take long at all. Believe me, it's worth it in the end.

Filo Pastry
Salmon Fillet
Cream Cheese
Baby Spinach Leaves
Melted Butter

I know that seems quite vague, but it really depends on how many you want to make (how many you can eat). Generally I buy a small smoked salmon fillet and make them until I have run out.
You need to work fast with filo, so make sure you are all organised before you begin.
Lay your filo out on a board and slice in half so you have two rectangles. Keep under a damp tea towel when not using.
Take one sheet and brush with melted butter, lay another sheet over top and brush with butter again. Lay one more layer on.
Place two decent dollops of cream cheese to one end and in the centre. Top with a few pieces of salmon – you don't need a lot in each one, and follow that with a couple of spinach leaves.
Fold both sides up and then roll the parcel as you would a sausage roll. Place on baking sheet, seal side down. Cut two slits in the top and brush with more melted butter.
Continue with remaining ingredients.
Bake in oven at 180°C keeping an eye on them. Once they start crisping you want to remove them.
Serve with a nice salad on the side.

Couscous Patties with Yoghurt Garlic Dressing

It may not sound that appealing, but it really is a great alternative to a meat pattie. You can have a meat free night, and it will still fill you up. Not to mention, it's quite cheap to make – you gotta love that!

It takes hardly any time to prepare and doesn't need any lengthy soaking. Serve it up with a salad and you have a lovely well rounded meal in no time at all!

2 C Couscous
2 ½ C Boiling Water
1 C Dates
70g Slivered Almonds
Salt and Pepper
1 Egg
125g Greek Yoghurt
3/4 Tsp Cumin
2 Cloves Garlic Crushed

Put couscous in a large bowl. Pour in boiling water. Cover with tea towel and leave to absorb.

In a small bowl combine yoghurt, garlic and cumin. Mix well and keep in fridge until patties are ready.

Once couscous has absorbed water, fluff it with a fork. Add chopped dates and almonds, salt and pepper, and egg. Mix well.
Form into small patties – it may help to wet your hands.

Cook in frying pan with a little oil until golden on each side.

Serve with dressing and a salad on the side.

Chorizo Risotto

Don't be frightened by the word "risotto". It's really not that hard. Time consuming – yes, a little. It does require frequent stirring, so you need to be on hand, not multi-tasking as so many of us do.

I have chosen chorizo because it has so much flavour, meaning you only need a fraction of the amount, again making it a cheaper meal.

2 Good quality Chorizo Sausages
¾ C Arborio Rice
2 C Beef Stock
2 Tbsp Butter
1 Onion diced
¼ C Parmesan Cheese

If your chorizo has a papery skin on it then peel this off. Slice into small chunks - about 1cm cubes.
Heat a large frying pan. Add chorizo and fry off. You will notice colour and fat oozing out of them – don't discard that, you will use that to cook the onions and rice in. Remove the chorizo once it has browned. Set aside.
Add onions to the pan and cook until softened, if pan is drying up then add a little oil.
Add rice and stir to coat with the juices. Slowly ladle beef stock in, one ladle at a time. You need to stir and let the rice absorb the liquid before adding more stock. This is the part that takes time. The constant stirring helps to release the starches in the rice, this is what gives it the creamy texture.
Once all the liquid has been added, test the rice to make sure it is cooked through – should take 20mins to get it right. Add the chorizo back into the pan, with the butter and parmesan. Stir again and make sure it's all mixed in.

Risotto is very filling so you don't need to have any side dishes. Just pile into a bowl and enjoy.

Pork Meatballs

If you have a peanut allergy, look away now. No wait! I didn't mean it! You can still make these without the peanuts and they are just as good. I love satay flavours, but having a son with a nut allergy means we don't get it very often. When I have a hankering for some satay, this is what I make. I just split the recipe in half and do satay for us adults, and non satay for the kids. Either way, there's plenty of flavour!

*Just remember if someone does have an allergy, you will need to cook these in separate pans, and use separate utensils.

400g Pork Mince
1 C Breadcrumbs
4 ½ Tbsp Soy Sauce
3 Tbsp Peanut Butter
1 Tbsp Sweet Chilli Sauce
1 tsp Ginger
½ Red Onion diced finely
Extra 1 ½ Tbsp Soy Sauce
1 ½ Tbsp Runny Honey

In a large bowl combine all ingredients (except second soy sauce and honey)
With wet hands, shape into small balls.
Heat oil in large frying pan and add balls. Brown on all sides.

Add second measure of soy sauce and swirl pan around.
Add honey and swirl around to coat. If you are able to, flip the meatballs in the pan. Keep tossing until they are coated and glossy.

These are lovely served by themselves or try them in a wrap with some salad.

Spaghetti Bolognese

Good old fashioned comfort food. Super tasty, and filling. The kids will love trying to swirl the spaghetti on their fork, or slurping it up like a worm. Who am I kidding? The adults love it too!

Topped with some grated cheese and a drizzle of olive oil, this dish is my "go to" recipe. Add a bit of parmesan to it as well and it makes it even better.

The way I do it, uses lentils as well, making it go further and again, cost less. Lentils are a great ingredient to have on hand in your pantry. They bulk up meals and stretch them – great for growing families, or when guests stop by at dinner time.

½ C Red Lentils
Water to cover
500g Mince
1 Tin Tomatoes
1 Tin Tomato Puree
Fresh Basil
1 Onion diced
1 Clove Garlic crushed
Spaghetti/Fettuccine Pasta
Grated Cheese

With a recipe like this, I generally use packet spaghetti pasta and cook as per instructions.
In a small saucepan, add lentils and water to cover. Boil for about 8 minutes to soften.
In a frying pan, heat a little oil. Add onions and cook until softened.
Add mince, breaking it up. Brown.
Add lentils, tomatoes, puree and basil. Simmer for 10 minutes.
Drain pasta.

To serve, swirl pasta onto plate and top with mince mix. Sprinkle with grated cheese and a drizzle of olive oil. If you feel so inclined, you can also add some fresh basil sprigs.

Mini Pizza

The kids love to help in the kitchen, especially when it involves pizza! Being mini, they are the perfect size for them to personalize their very own pizza. You'd be surprised how much more likely they are to eat toppings if they have put them on themselves. It gives them a chance to experiment too, which helps make them confident in the kitchen.

I have a bread-maker, so I quite often make my own pizza dough, you can also use tortillas, pre-bought bases, scone mix shaped into a base, or whatever takes your fancy.

When the kids are helping, I put toppings in small bowls for them to choose from. You have to be prepared for a bit of mess with this! Once they have picked out what they want, then pop them all in the oven for around

10-15minutes at 180ºC

Topping suggestions:

*Chicken, cranberry/apricot/barbeque sauce, camembert, cream cheese, grated cheese, onion

*Salami, kransky, tomato/barbeque sauce, diced ham, bacon, onion, grated cheese

*Tomato sauce, fresh basil, mozzarella cheese

*Cream cheese, salmon, spinach, grated cheese

*Cream cheese, capsicum, onion, tomato, olives, mushroom, grated cheese

Dessert

We all need a bit of sweetness in our lives. This section has a few recipes
that look impressive and are easier to make than you would expect.

Apricot Pie

We are lucky enough to have an apricot tree at our house. I never knew apricots could be so juicy and sweet!

One thing with fruit trees though, is that a lot of fruit ripens at the same time, and they don't last too long after that. So this recipe is perfect for those extra apricots!

You can use a proper pie dish to cook it in, but I quite like it to look a little more rustic. There really is no "right" way to do it. Here is my interpretation of an apricot pie.

8 Apricots
Splash of Water
½ tsp Cinnamon
2 Tbsp Sugar
2 Tbsp Flour
2 tsp Butter
Two Sheets of Short Sweet Pastry

I don't bother to peel the apricots for this, the skin kind of melts into the pulp anyway, and that's where all the sweetness and goodness is.
Chop the apricots and remove the centre. Put them in a saucepan with the water, sugar and cinnamon. Simmer until it is soft and pulpy.
Add the butter and stir until melted.
Add flour to thicken it slightly.

Using the first sheet of pastry, line your pie dish/bowl/baking tray.
Spoon the apricot mix onto the pastry.
Top with the second sheet of pastry – you can cover completely and seal with a fork, or cut out strips/shapes and position those on top.
Brush a little milk over the lid and pop in the oven at 180^0C for 20 minutes or until pastry is golden.

Leave in dish for a few minutes before slicing. Delicious served with cream or ice cream.

Pavlova with Chocolate Mousse

This recipe came to me while having dinner with friends one night. We had been discussing our favourite desserts and pavlova came up. One said that he'd tried it once with chocolate inside the pav but couldn't figure out how they did it.

After a few attempts at reconstructing that, I came up with this recipe as a substitute. It was well received!

Both parts of this dessert are fabulous on their own as well, but extra decadent when you combine them.

Pavlova
3 Egg Whites
1 C Caster Sugar
1 tsp Vanilla Paste
1 tsp Malt Vinegar
3 tsp Cornflour

Chocolate Mousse
3 Egg Yolks
300ml Cream
3 Tbsp Caster Sugar
1 C Dark Chocolate Drops

Egg whites are best at room temperature.
Make sure your bowl is completely dry before adding them.

Beat egg whites until thick. Gradually add in the caster sugar (still beating). It should be glossy and thick.
In a small bowl combine vanilla, vinegar and cornflour and then add to the bowl and beat again.

If making just a pavlova, then spoon onto a baking sheet in one circle approx. 20cm. If making with the chocolate mousse, then you want to split it into two circles. Try to keep them about the same size.

Put in oven heated to 150^0C turn down to 120^0C and bake for 30minutes. It should have a very light brown colour to it. Leave it to cool in the oven.

Continued next page

To make the chocolate mousse:

Place chocolate in a large glass bowl and set aside.

In a small bowl whisk egg yolks and sugar until pale and creamy.

Heat ¼ C of the cream in a small saucepan, do not let it boil.
Slowly pour cream into egg mix (whisking the whole time). Pour mixture back into the saucepan and continue heating until it coats the back of a wooden spoon.

Using a fine sieve, pour cream and egg into the chocolate (this way if any egg has cooked, it won't be added to the mousse.
Stir until smooth.

Whip remaining cream and add to the mousse one spoonful at a time, slowly folding to incorporate without losing all the air.

Cover and leave to set in fridge – at least 1hour.

If making the whole dessert, when ready to serve, place one pavlova on your serving board, spoon mousse on top and then place the second pavlova over the mousse.
You can decorate with more mousse or whipped cream and I like to make a berry coulis using frozen berries and a little sugar to spoon over top.

Homemade Ice Cream

Don't worry, you don't have to rush out and buy a fancy machine to make this! I made this recipe up before I knew you could get those. It's such a simple recipe and super tasty. Be prepared for sweetness though. It's one of those desserts that you only need a small amount of.

You can make it a more adult pudding by adding a few tablespoons of your favourite schnapps, or just keep it the same for a family friendly one. Believe me, the kids love this one!

1 Tin Condensed Milk
300ml Cream
1 Packet Choc Thins Biscuits
1 Tsp Vanilla Paste

There's really nothing simpler.
Beat cream until soft peaks are forming. Add condensed milk and vanilla and beat to combine.
Put choc thins in a bag and bash with your rolling pin – take out all those frustrations on it! It can be as crumbly or as chunky as you like.
Fold into the cream mixture.
Pour into a cleaned out ice cream container. Put lid on and pop in the freezer for an hour.

Remove and give it another beat, then put back in the freezer for a further 2 hours.

It is best served on the same day as made, but does last if you are lucky enough to have leftovers!

Chocolate Cheesecake Pie

Chocolate and cheesecake. Two of the best things to eat!

1 Quantity of Chocolate Mousse
1 Pack Choc Thins
100g Melted Butter
125g Cream Cheese
150ml Cream
1 tsp Vanilla Paste
¼ C Caster Sugar
1 Flake Bar
1 tsp Gelatine
2 Tbsp Boiling Water

Blitz choc thins and butter in a blender. Press into a spring-form pan. Pop in the fridge to set.

Beat cream cheese, sugar, vanilla and gelatine until smooth. Fold in cream and crumbled flake bar.

Pour onto base and put in fridge to set for an hour.

Make chocolate mousse, (see page 64) and smooth over top of cheesecake and leave in fridge for at least another hour to set.

To serve, sprinkle a little cocoa over top and enjoy!

Semifreddo

Another simple dessert to make that will impress your guests.

I have used Greek yoghurt in place of mascarpone, which makes it slightly better for you – there's still cream and chocolate in it so it's not completely guilt free!

It does require a few hours in the freezer so you need to be prepared for that, but the actual making it part, is super easy.

125g Greek Yoghurt
250ml Cream
2 Tbsp Maple Syrup
4 Tbsp Icing Sugar
½ C Cream Cheese
½ C Dark Chocolate
½ C Raspberries
70g Almonds

In a large bowl, combine yoghurt, cream, syrup, icing sugar and cream cheese (room temperature) and beat until smooth and thickening.
Fold in the chocolate, raspberries and almonds.
Get a metal loaf tin, grease it, and line it with cling film – this needs to be hanging over the edge too.
Pour mixture into loaf tin and fold the cling film over the top.
Make sure it is completely covered with cling film. Place in freezer for 3 hours.

When ready to serve, remove from freezer and let it sit for around 15 minutes to soften it. Lift out of the tin using the cling film. Unwrap the top and flip it up and onto serving platter.
Lift off the rest of the cling film.
Using a sharp knife, slice into 2cm slices.

You can serve with a little coulis over it, or just on its own.

Ambrosia

This is a great recipe to make with the kids. They can mix it any way they like and it will still end up tasting fabulous! There's really no skill involved in this one.

You can serve it up in individual bowls by itself, or top a pavlova (see page 65) with it. Crumble up some meringue and mix it through or even add some schnapps to it – keep this for the adults only though!

300ml Cream
2 C Berry Yoghurt
1 C Fresh Berries
1 C Mini Marshmallows
½ C White Chocolate Buttons
½ C Dark Chocolate Buttons
3 Tbsp Icing Sugar

Beat cream with sugar until thick and firm peaks have formed (don't let it turn into butter though!).
Fold in remaining ingredients.
Serve!

If you want to add some alcohol, I would add it to the berries and let them soak in it first. A fruity schnapps or a chocolate liqueur would work well.

Rhubarb and Apricot Crumble

Not only do we grow apricots, we also grow our own rhubarb. Normally I would do rhubarb crumble on its own or with apples, but I decided to do something different this time and it paid off. The combination of the two is just delicious.
The colour is more vibrant and appealing too.

3 Apricots
1 ½ C Rhubarb
3 tsp Sugar
½ C Brown Sugar
½ C Oats
½ C Wholemeal Flour
½ tsp Cinnamon
75g Butter

Put apricots, rhubarb and sugar in a saucepan and simmer until soft. Pour into greased pudding dish.

In a bowl add remaining ingredients to make the crumble. Rub the butter in to make a breadcrumb.
Sprinkle crumble mix over fruit and pop in oven at 180^0C for 30 minutes or untIl bubbling.

Serve with yoghurt or cream.

Just to say...

A big thank you to each and every one of you reading this, for without you, this book would not have been possible. I hope you have enjoyed reading and experimenting with these recipes, as much as I enjoyed writing them for you.

I'd also like to thank my husband and children for being my guinea pigs and providing endless support. I love you all so much.

And of course, to my sister Tegan, for making the trip to my house daily to photograph each meal and make my food look even more delicious! I could not have done this without her. She was the one to push me to write a blog and give me the confidence to go further. This has been a wonderful journey, with its fair share of mishaps in the process. I think though, it has turned into a success. Something I can be proud of. I am glad to be able to share my love of cooking and entertaining with you, and perhaps I have inspired you to try something new.

Thank you all!
Stacey xxx

www.calamityjaynefoodie.blogspot.co.nz
www.facebook.com/calamityjaynefoodie